LODI MEMORIAL LIBRARY, NJ

3 9139 09038084 2

DISCARD

D1294902

EVERYDAY HISTORY

LIFE IN

ANCIENT GREECE

SARAH RIDLEY

Property of
Lodi Memorial Library

A+

Smart Apple Media

Published by Smart Apple Media, an imprint of Black Rabbit Books
P.O. Box 3263, Mankato, Minnesota 56002
www.smartapplemedia.com

U.S. publication copyright © 2016 Smart Apple Media. All rights reserved. International copyright
reserved in all countries. No part of this book may be reproduced in any form without written
permission from the publisher.

Published by arrangement with Watts Publishing, London.

Library of Congress Cataloging-in-Publication Data
Ridley, Sarah.
  Life in Ancient Greece / Sarah Ridley.
      pages cm. — (Everyday history)
  Includes index.
   ISBN 978-1-59920-950-0
  eISBN 978-1-68071-005-2
  1. Greece—Civilization—To 146 B.C.—Juvenile literature. I. Title.
  DF77.R525 2015
  938—dc23
                                    2013033417

Picture credits:

Ancient Art and Architecture Collection: 4t, 24t, 24b, 25b.
Courtesy of the Trustees of the British Museum:
front cover bc & br, 8t, 10t, 12t, 16t, 18t, 20t, 22t, 26t, 30t.
Werner Forman Archive: 28t.
Michael Holford: 6 (all), 7 (all), 14t.

Printed in the United States by CG Book Printers
North Mankato, Minnesota

PO 1729
3-2015

CONTENTS

WHO WERE THE ANCIENT GREEKS?

The land of Greece was divided by mountains and included many islands. In ancient times, this made it difficult to rule as one country. Most ancient Greeks lived in independent city-states. Each state governed itself from the main town in the area and controlled the surrounding land. The city-states were often at war with each other. This book looks at life in the city-states from around 800 to 350 BC.

This gold mask was found by archaeologists at Mycenae on the Greek mainland. It dates from around 1550–1500 BC.

Before this time, two earlier civilizations lived in Greece—the Minoans and the Mycenaeans. The Minoans built their center on the island of Crete. Later, the Mycenaeans, who had lived on the Greek mainland, became rich and powerful by trading in the Mediterranean. After the Mycenaean period, the area had no powerful rulers for a few hundred years. This period of time is sometimes known as the Dark Ages, which ended ca. 800 BC.

IMPORTANT DATES FROM THE TIME OF THE ANCIENT GREEKS

2000–1500 BC

The Minoan civilization rises and falls. It is replaced by the Mycenaeans.

1500–1100 BC

The rise of the Mycenaeans. The invasion of Crete, the Trojan War, and the collapse of the Mycenaean civilization.

1100–800 BC

The Dark Ages.
800 The rise of city-states.

800–600 BC

Homer writes the *Iliad* and the *Odyssey*. Colonies are founded in Asia Minor and around the Mediterranean. Coins are introduced.
776 First Olympic Games.

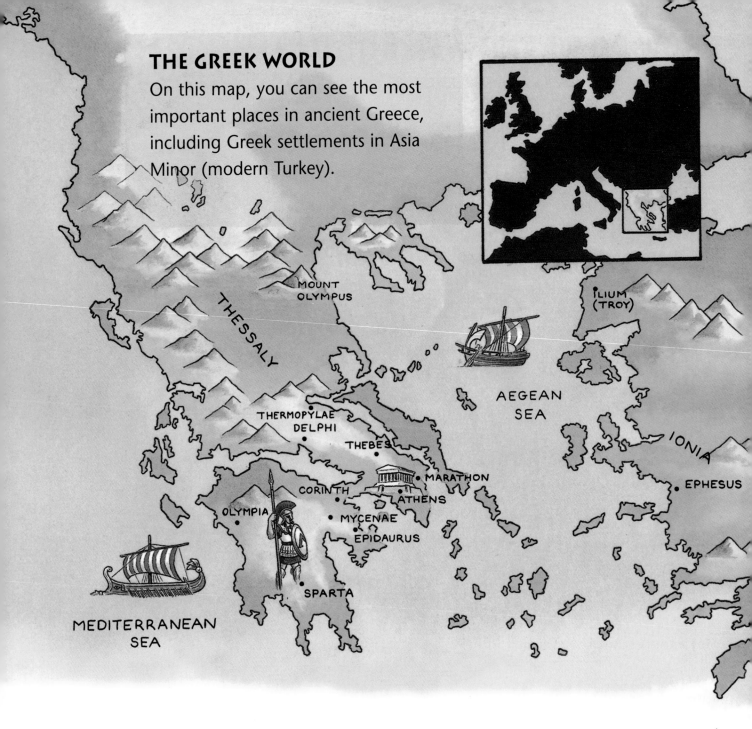

THE GREEK WORLD

On this map, you can see the most important places in ancient Greece, including Greek settlements in Asia Minor (modern Turkey).

MOUNT OLYMPUS

THESSALY

ILIUM (TROY)

THERMOPYLAE
DELPHI
THEBES
CORINTH
OLYMPIA
ATHENS
MARATHON
MYCENAE
EPIDAURUS
SPARTA

AEGEAN SEA

IONIA

EPHESUS

MEDITERRANEAN SEA

600–480 BC

The beginnings of democracy in Athens.
490–479 Persian wars.

480–400 BC

The age of Pericles:
447–432 The Parthenon is built at Athens.
The Classical period:
431–404 War between Athens and Sparta.

400–300 BC

The rise of Philip of Macedon.
336 The death of Philip and succession of Alexander the Great of Macedon.

336–323 Alexander the Great wins an empire stretching from Egypt to northern India.
323 The death of Alexander the Great.

5

HOW DO WE KNOW ABOUT THE ANCIENT GREEKS?

The ancient Greeks have left us many clues that tell us about their daily life. We know about them from reading their writings, from the impressive buildings still standing today, and from the evidence of archaeological excavations. You can see Greek objects, especially vases and sculptures, in museums worldwide.

This Greek sculpture is one of a number that survive. It may represent the god Apollo.

STANDING STRUCTURES

Some of the temples, theaters, athletics' tracks, and other public buildings built by the ancient Greeks survive today. To see some of the best temples, visit the Acropolis, a high rocky area in Athens. Another important site is Delphi. Archaeologists have discovered roads, temples, and a stadium for sporting competitions here.

All these buildings have survived earthquakes, wind, and rain for thousands of years, showing the skill of the architects and sculptors who built them.

The Acropolis, Athens

ARCHAEOLOGY

Archaeologists continue to excavate many ancient Greek sites. The objects they find, such as pottery, metalwork, jewelry, and the foundations of many buildings, tell us about life in Greece. Clothes and furniture do not usually survive.

POTTERY

We know a great deal about life in ancient Greece from the pictures painted on Greek pots. These show clothes, furniture, and people going about their everyday lives. Many pots were found in tombs that had been left as offerings to the gods.

LITERATURE

This is a sculpture (*right*) of the poet Homer (lived 8 BC), who authored the *Iliad* and the *Odyssey*. Few original Greek writings survive. However, the Romans, who made Greece part of their empire, created many copies of Greek books. In turn, these were copied by monks in medieval times.

FARMING AND FISHING

Most Greek men were farmers growing what they could in the dry, rocky soil. Olive trees flourished as they do today. We can see how the ancient Greeks harvested the olives by looking at the vase painting (*right*). Two men knock the olives down while a third shakes the branches. Another man collects the olives in a basket.

FARMING, FISHING AND HUNTING

Farmers grew barley and wheat to make bread and porridge. Other crops included beans, lentils, onions, leeks, and garlic. Farmers also kept sheep and goats. The goats provided milk for cheese as well as animal skins to make clothes. The sheep's wool was woven into cloth for clothes and furnishings. On the hills, people grew olive and fruit trees and grapevines.

Fishermen used wooden boats to catch fish—the main food for most people. Rich men and women ate meat more often as the young men liked to hunt deer or boar to eat on special occasions.

This beautiful dish was probably used to serve fish dishes. People dipped cooked fish into a rich, spicy sauce that was held in the center of the dish.

A busy family farm in the countryside.

THE GREEK FARM

Most Greek farms were small and run by one family with a few farmhands and slaves. Some wealthier city people employed farm managers to look after their farms in the countryside.

Farmhouses, like town houses, were built around a central courtyard. Some homes had defensive towers to protect them from attack in times of war.

Farmers used donkeys fitted with baskets to transport goods to market. The baskets were loaded with produce such as cheese, vegetables, fruit, olives, honey, or jars of wine.

THE GREEK HOME

Greek homes, whether in the town or the countryside, were built around a central courtyard. The Greek household could include married children and relatives.

Wealthy men liked to invite their friends to the house for drinking parties. Wine, mixed with water, was served from drinking bowls like this one (*left*). The bowl, perched on a painted stand, was close enough for the guests to refill their cups.

THE HOUSE

Greek houses, unlike temples, were built from mud bricks rather than stone. A layer of stones was used as a base or foundation.

The roof had clay tiles. The windows were small and high up with wooden shutters. Doors were also made of wood, which was expensive because it was in short supply.

The courtyard design gave the family a private area in the center of the home where children could play while women worked out of the sun. A family altar was usually in the center of the courtyard.

LIGHTING

Small clay or bronze lamps burnt olive oil to produce a flickering, and probably smoky, light. Most people went to bed when the sun set.

Resting on cushions on top of couches, men enjoy a drinking party. The slave girl keeps the men supplied with food and drink.

The Greeks had less furniture than we do today. Low, wooden couches matched low tables and stools. Chests, boxes, and baskets kept everything tidy.

Chair

Table

Stool

THE MEN'S ROOM

Men and women had separate areas inside the house. The men's room was called the *andron*, which is where they held parties for their friends or business contacts. The andron was often near the entrance of the house, so drunken guests could leave without bumping into any of the women of the household.

Property of
Lodi Memorial Library

11

WOMEN'S LIVES

Greek women spent most of their lives in the home looking after the household and making cloth. This painted clay object, called an *epinetron*, shows Greek women working with wool. The epinetron protected the woman's knee while she pulled wool into strands suitable for spinning. Both spinning and weaving were considered important tasks.

THE WOMEN'S ROOM

Most Greek homes had a special room called the *gynaekonitis*. Women of the house gathered here to work, entertain female friends, and be with their children. Women spun wool and wove cloth here to make clothes for the family and furnishings, such as curtains and cushion covers, for the house.

Women's lives were controlled by the head of the household—their husband, father, or brother. Women could not take part in politics and rarely had a job in the outside world. Girls married young, at the age of 13 or 14, usually to an older man chosen for them by their father.

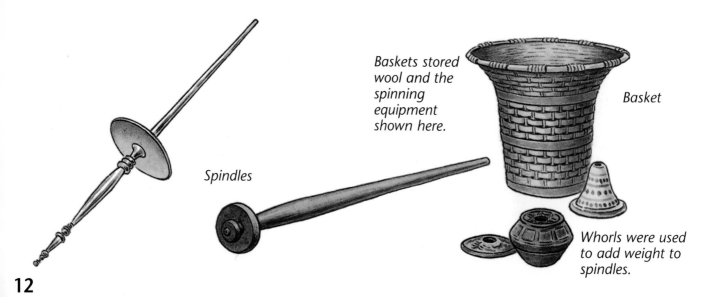

Baskets stored wool and the spinning equipment shown here.

Basket

Spindles

Whorls were used to add weight to spindles.

Three young wives work together using an epinetron, a loom, and a spindle and distaff.

Archaeologists have discovered many cosmetic containers. Greek women used creams to protect their skin from the sun, and used makeup to create a pale look.

SPINNING AND WEAVING

A Greek woman used a spindle and distaff to spin wool. Holding the distaff, with its bundle of wool, in her left hand, she drew a thread from the wool and wound it around the spindle. Then she let the spindle drop toward the ground, twisting the thread as it went. The twisted thread could be woven into cloth by using a loom propped up against the wall.

CLOTHES AND JEWELRY

Greek clothes were loose and flowing as shown on the clay figure of a woman (*right*). She is wearing a *chiton*, a long tunic, along with the other main Greek garment, a cloak called a *himation*. Clay figures were made as ornaments for the home or gifts for the temple. These give us clear images of the clothes Greek people wore.

THE CHITON

The chiton was a rectangular piece of fine wool or linen that had been woven by the women of the household (see pages 12–13). It was folded or pinned into place and gathered at the waist by a soft belt.

MYSTERY OBJECT

These clay containers were found in the women's room and smelled pleasant. Can you guess what they contained? (Answer on page 32.)

Men and women wore ankle-length chitons. Slaves and children wore chitons short to allow them to work and play. Chitons came in pretty colors, though these were more expensive

WOMEN'S HAIRSTYLES

Unless women were slaves, they wore their hair long. Before they were married, they wore it in long ringlets. After that they piled their hair up on their heads with ribbons and hair decorations. When the women went out, they pulled their cloaks up over the head.

A Greek family wear the clothes of the time. Sometimes men wore just the himation (cloak), as shown here.

Rich women wore a lot of gold and silver jewelry, especially dangling earrings, bracelets, and rings.

CHILDHOOD AND GAMES

Paintings on vases and toys show us that children had plenty to play with in ancient Greece. This pig rattle (*right*) is made of clay and probably belonged to the child of a wealthy family. The person who made it sealed pieces of dry clay inside the pig to create the rattling noise.

TO LIVE OR DIE

When a baby was born, the mother handed the child to her husband. He decided whether the baby should live or die. If the baby was weak or deformed, he might decide to let it die by leaving it outside in the cold. Sometimes, other families rescued these babies and brought them up as slaves.

CHILDHOOD

Once accepted into the family, babies were well cared for. The children of wealthy families learned to play musical instruments, received education (see pages 18–19), and played games. Poor children worked hard from their early years by helping their parents at work or in the home. At the age of 12, a religious ceremony marked the end of childhood. Children brought their toys to the temple and left them as offerings to the gods.

The painting on this small wine jar shows a boy sitting in his high chair, which also served as a potty!

Children play with clay toys, a spinning top, a hoop, and a pet dog.

TOYS AND GAMES

Greek children played many of the games that children play today—Blind Man's Bluff, tag, and ball games. They rolled hoops, spun spinning tops, and pulled each other around in go-carts. They also played board games and a throwing game using knuckle bones. Many clay toys survive but the wooden and cloth ones have disappeared.

The clay doll, play figures, and balls shown here were once painted in bright colors.

GOING TO SCHOOL

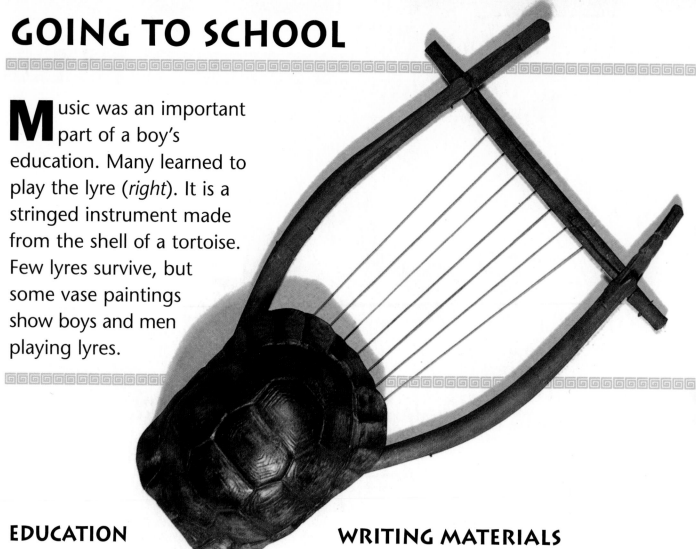

Music was an important part of a boy's education. Many learned to play the lyre (*right*). It is a stringed instrument made from the shell of a tortoise. Few lyres survive, but some vase paintings show boys and men playing lyres.

EDUCATION

Most poor children received no education. Boys, whose families were better-off, could attend schools in cities and towns. They started school at the age of 7 and stayed until the age of 15. They then went on to a gymnasium to concentrate on athletics.

While the girls stayed at home, their mothers taught them how to run the household, spin, and weave cloth. A few girls from wealthy families were taught how to read and write.

WRITING MATERIALS

Pupils wrote with a stylus on reusable wax tablets. They also used a reed pen dipped in ink to write on papyrus scrolls, which were lengths of paper made from reeds.

Papyrus scroll and reed pen

SCHOOL

A family slave took the boys of the household to school and back. In class, the pupils sat on stools gathered around the teacher. He taught them reading, writing, and math. They also memorized the works of famous poets, such as Homer. The afternoons were devoted to sports and athletics.

Greek classes were small with just six or seven pupils. The teacher is using a papyrus scroll.

THE ALPHABET

The Phoenicians—a people who traded with the Greeks—brought the alphabet to Greece in about 800 BC. The following words were written by the playwright, Aeschylus:

"I have brought you up, and want to grow old with you beside me."

A A	**B** B	**Γ** G	**Δ** D	**E** E	**Z** Z
H EE	**Θ** TH	**I** I	**K** K	**Λ** L	**M** M
N N	**Ξ** X/KS	**O** O	**Π** P	**P** R	**Σ** S
T T	**Y** U	**Φ** F/PH	**X** CH	**Ψ** PS	**Ω** OH

ἐγω σ' εθρεψα,
συν δε γηραναι
θελω

CRAFTSMEN AND MARKETS

Around the market place, or *agora*, craftsmen made goods to sell from shops at the front of their workshops. The painting on the drinking cup (*right*) shows a cobbler at work, as he cuts up pieces of leather to make boots and sandals. Other craftsmen made goods such as jewelry, weapons, furniture, and pottery.

POTTERS

Potters outnumbered all the other types of craftsmen. They worked in groups of five or six people, usually men, although some women were involved, especially in painting pots.

There was a room where they made the pots, sometimes with the help of a slave who turned the potter's wheel. When the pots were dry, they were painted. Many paintings show beautiful scenes of everyday life or events in the lives of the gods and goddesses. Another room at the front served as a shop where customers came to buy household jars, cups and crockery.

NAMES OF SOME POT SHAPES:
Amphora—two-handled jar for storing wine
Kylix—wide drinking cup with two handles
Oinochoe—wine jug
Krater—large pot for mixing water and wine

Amphora

Oinochoe

Kylix

Krater

A Greek housewife carefully examines some cloth before making her purchase in the agora.

THE AGORA

Every Greek town had an agora, or market place, where people came every day to shop, meet friends, or do some business. It was a large open space near the center of the town. Market traders set up stalls to sell goods or farm produce, such as vegetables, cheese, olives, and fruit, brought in from the countryside. Craftsmen's workshops lined the streets around the agora.

MONEY

Coins came to Greece in the late seventh century BC. At first, coins were too valuable to be used for everyday shopping, so people continued to barter (exchange) goods with each other. Later, coins made from a cheaper metal were used in the market place.

SPORTS AND GAMES

The Greeks held sporting festivals in honor of particular gods and goddesses. Athletes competed in various events, including running races, wrestling, and discus-throwing. The bronze discus (*left*) belonged to a Greek athlete named Exodias. His name, and the fact that he won a competition with it, are written on the discus.

THE GREEK GAMES

The Olympic Games, held at Olympia in honor of the god Zeus and the Panathenaic Games, held in Athens in honor of the goddess Athena, were the most famous events. Held every four years, athletes and spectators traveled from across Greece to attend. As the Greek city-states were often at war with one other, a truce (peace) was called to allow the Olympic Games to be held.

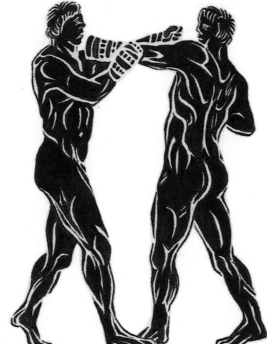

PRIZES

Because the games were religious occasions, athletes did not receive cash prizes for coming in first. At the Olympics, each winner received a wreath made of olive branches. At the Panathenaic Games, the best athletes were awarded olive oil in a big pot. A picture on one side of the pot depicted the event that had been won. In this case, wrestling (*left*), and on the other side was a painting of the goddess Athena.

Athletes prepare for the Olympic games at an open-air training ground.

CONTESTANTS

Boys were taught sporting skills to help them become fit soldiers in adult life. Most greek towns had special training grounds and wrestling schools where boys went to exercise and compete.

The best athletes went to the games (*left*). They competed naked in a stadium and watched by thousands of spectators. Successful athletes became famous in their home towns.

MYSTERY OBJECT

How do you think this metal object was used? It was used by athletes after competing, to help them get clean. (Answer on page 32.)

GOING TO THE THEATER

Greek people enjoyed a day out at the theater. The actors wore masks that showed what sort of character they were playing. This clay mask (*right*) was used as a decoration, but actors wore something very similar made of stiffened linen. The mouth of the mask was large to allow the actor's voice to be heard.

THE PLAYS

The theater in Athens started out as hymns and dances to the god of wine, Dionysus. This developed into play competitions as part of a spring festival for Dionysus. The plays were divided into tragedies and comedies. As they were always about the lives of the gods and goddesses, the audience nearly always knew what would happen.

A theater survives, almost intact, at Epidauros in Greece. It could seat 14,000 people.

We still have copies of plays by four famous Greek playwrights: Aeschylus, Sophocles, Euripides, and Aristophanes.

The large semicircular space in the theater was called the orchestra. The actors performed the play, using the buildings behind the orchestra to change costumes.

A BIG DAY OUT

People spent the whole day at the theater, watching play after play. They brought cushions to sit on and a packed lunch. While the best seats were at the front, the shape of the theater meant that even the people at the back could hear what the actors were saying. Only three actors at a time were allowed to speak, but a chorus of actors described the action on and off stage.

These are reconstructions of Greek masks. They are made from stiffened linen with real hair for the beard and head.

IN THE ARMY

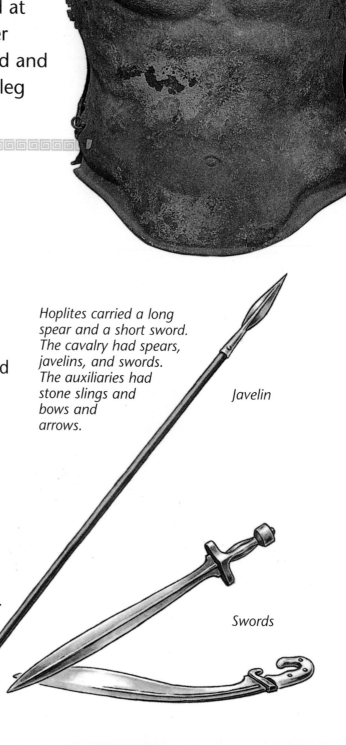

Men were expected to join the army when their city-state was at war. The foot soldiers, called hoplites, usually had to buy their own armor and weapons, including a breastplate similar to this bronze one (*right*). It was fastened at the sides with leather straps. Other equipment included a round shield and a helmet. Some hoplites also had leg guards called greaves.

BATTLE TACTICS

Hoplites fought shoulder to shoulder in a battle formation called a *phalanx*. It consisted of eight rows of soldiers protected by shields. Although the phalanx moved slowly around the battlefield, it was very successful in battle. The hoplites were greatly feared by foreign armies. In 490 BC, the hoplites spectacularly defeated the invading Persian army, killing thousands of Persians and chasing the rest back to their ships.

Other Greek soldiers included cavalrymen, who rode horses, and auxiliary soldiers. These were the poor men who could not afford hoplite armor. Sometimes they were used to protect the phalanx.

Hoplites carried a long spear and a short sword. The cavalry had spears, javelins, and swords. The auxiliaries had stone slings and bows and arrows.

Javelin

Swords

26

A young woman says good-bye to her soldier husband as he goes off to war.

THE LIFE OF A SOLDIER

In Athens and other Greek cities, boys trained to be soldiers between the ages of 18 and 20. After that, they could be called to join the army when necessary to fight for their city-state. War was a normal part of ancient Greek life, and battles took place almost every year.

Only the city of Sparta, a long-time enemy of Athens, had a professional army. The life of a Spartan soldier was very hard. Boys left their families as early as the age of seven for a life of army training and harsh living conditions. They seldom saw their families.

Helmets came in different shapes. This one is the Corinthian type. Made of bronze, it covers the entire head except for the eyes and mouth.

WORSHIPPING THE GODS

The Greeks worshipped many gods and goddesses and built temples in their honor. Some of these temples survive, such as the Parthenon (*right*) on the Acropolis, Athens. It was built between 447–432 BC for the goddess Athena.

GODS AND GODDESSES

Gods and goddesses were part of the everyday lives of the ancient Greeks. People believed that the gods would treat them well, and that life would go well, if they offered prayers and gifts to the gods.

The twelve most important gods were believed to live on the top of a high mountain in northern Greece called Mount Olympus. Zeus was the king of the gods and carried a thunderbolt to show his power over the heavens. His wife, Hera, was the protector of women and marriage.

ARCHITECTURAL STYLES

Greek temples were built in two main styles: Doric and Ionic. Doric columns have simple tops (capitals) while Ionic columns have more decoration and slender columns.

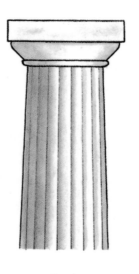

Doric

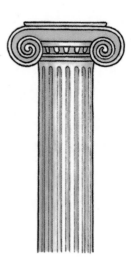

Ionic

A cow is led to the altar for sacrifice. The Greeks believed that animal sacrifices pleased the gods and goddesses.

A third architectural style, called Corinthian, was developed by the Romans. Its capitals were decorated with carved acanthus leaves.

Corinthian

TEMPLES AND SACRIFICE

Temples were sacred buildings and considered the homes of the gods. Inside, most temples usually had a huge statue of the god or goddess to whom the temple was dedicated. The Parthenon (*page 28, top left*), had a huge gold and ivory statue of the goddess Athena. The altar for sacrificing animals was outside the temple. People gathered here on important occasions to make offerings to their god or goddess.

DEATH AND BURIAL

Funerals were important events in ancient Greece. When someone died, the family gathered to grieve and pray to the gods. Using sweet-smelling oil kept in slender flasks called *lekythoi* (*right*), the body was prepared for burial. The lekythoi flasks often were buried with the dead person as an offering to the gods.

A tall, spindly type of pot, called a loutrophoros *(left), is often found in ancient Greek burial areas. This type of pot was used to carry water for the special bath a woman took before her marriage, and it was also used as a marker on the graves of unmarried women.*

MOURNERS

Friends and relatives came to show respect and say farewell to the dead person, who was laid out on a couch with a wreath around his or her head. When it was time for the funeral, a long procession accompanied the body. The family placed food and favorite objects in the grave, believing that these items could pass across to the underworld.

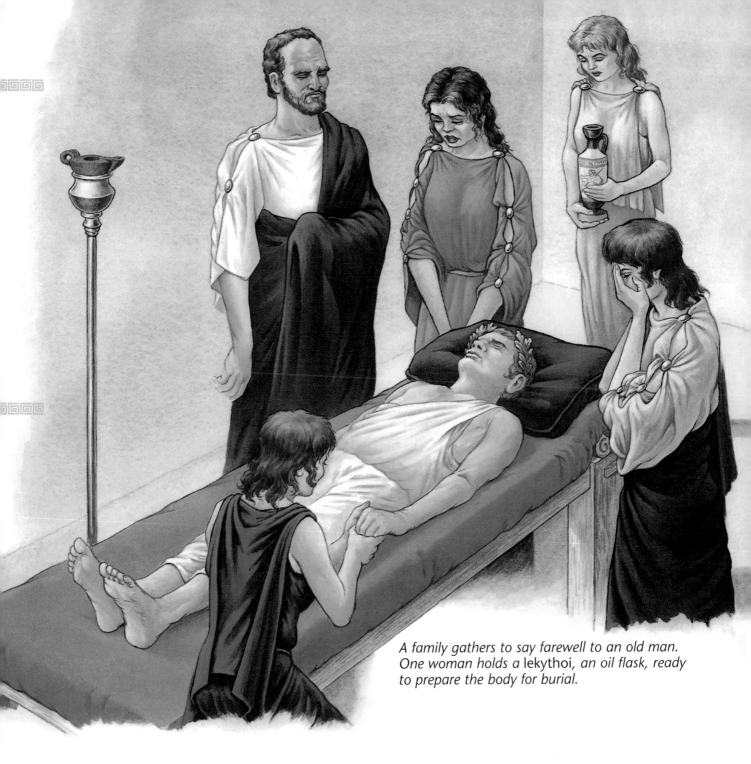

A family gathers to say farewell to an old man. One woman holds a lekythoi, *an oil flask, ready to prepare the body for burial.*

THE UNDERWORLD

Greeks believed the spirits of dead people went to the underworld, which was ruled over by the god Pluto, also known as Hades. Spirits were taken there by Charon, the ferryman, who rowed them across the River Styx.

Relatives often placed a coin on the dead body to pay Charon for this service. It was important that the dead person's spirit reached the underworld. Otherwise, the spirit would remain on Earth as a ghost haunting the living.

INDEX

ANSWERS TO MYSTERY OBJECT BOXES

Page 14: These clay objects are perfume containers. Perfume containers came in all sorts of shapes, from birds to helmets.

Page 23: This is a strigil. After sport, men rubbed their bodies with olive oil and then scraped oil and dirt off their bodies using a strigil.